FELIX MENDELSSOHN BARTHOLDY

SYMPHONY No. 5

D minor/d-Moll/Ré mineur
Op. 107
'Reformation'

T0081281

Ernst Eulenburg Ltd

London · Mainz · Madrid · New York · Paris · Prague · Tokyo · Toronto · Zürich

CONTENTS

Preface III

Vorwort V

  I. Andante – Allegro con fuoco 1

 II. Allegro vivace 47

III. Andante 56

IV. Chorale: Ein' feste Burg. Andante con moto – Allegro maestoso . . . 59

© 2015 Ernst Eulenburg & Co GmbH, Mainz
for Europe excluding the British Isles
Ernst Eulenburg Ltd, London
for all other countries

All rights reserved.
No part of this publication may be reproduced, stored in a retrieval system,
or transmitted in any form or by any means,
electronic, mechanical, photocopying, recording or otherwise,
without the prior written permission of the publisher:

Ernst Eulenburg Ltd
48 Great Marlborough Street
London W1F 7BB

PREFACE

Mendelssohn first mentions this symphony in a letter he wrote to his family from Wales in September 1829, as he was coming to the end of the seven-month stay in Britain that inspired the overture *The Hebrides* and the *Scottish Symphony*. His intention was to compose something for the tercentenary celebrations of the Confession of Augsburg, a key moment in the Protestant Reformation, when on 25 June 1530 the Catholic Emperor Charles V was presented with the 28 articles that outlined the basis of the Lutheran faith.

There was no specific commission for a symphony, however, and perhaps Mendelssohn's Jewish origins would have counted against him if any musical celebration had actually taken place. In any event, although he returned to Berlin and completed the symphony with his customary speed and enthusiasm by May 1830, he almost immediately set off on a long tour of southern Germany, Italy and France. A performance was planned in Paris at the beginning of 1832 under François-Antoine Habeneck, but to Mendelssohn's annoyance the French players refused to co-operate, finding it too full of counterpoint and with too few tunes for their taste. This was essentially also the reaction of the Berlin poet and critic Ludwig Rellstab after Mendelssohn conducted the first performance there on 15 November 1832. Rellstab was impressed, but went on to say:

We should like it better if the composer did not insist so much on colossal features, as beautiful as they may be, if he did not orchestrate so over-richly; and, finally, if he gave melody precedence over the beauties of daringly combined harmony. In addition, he rarely shows us smiling heavens, it is nearly always stormy and thundery.[1]

In the odd way that composers sometimes have of turning against their own works,

Mendelssohn did nothing further to promote the symphony or have it published. His attitude may have less to do with the work's musical qualities than with his strict view of what a symphony should or should not be. A clue lies in a further remark by Rellstab: 'It can never be the aim of music to represent sensuously an event that belongs almost exclusively to the world of pure thought.'[2] There is a clear programmatic, even narrative, plan to the symphony, as it represents the triumph of 'enlightened' Protestantism over 'obscurantist' Catholicism. Whatever Mendelssohn's religious views – and we know he was very liberal and broadminded in this respect – his musical beliefs included a sharp distinction between 'illustrative' and 'pure' music, and he may well have come to feel that what was appropriate for an overture or a work with text like an oratorio was out of place in a symphony, which should deal only with abstract musical processes. Whatever lay behind his discomfort, it hardly justifies his reported description of the first movement as 'a fat bristly animal' or his purported wish to burn the whole thing. The symphony was published only after his death with the number five, although strictly speaking it is his second symphony in order of composition.

The symphony's introduction begins in a mood of solemnity with the sort of counterpoint that in Mendelssohn's time was associated with the style of Palestrina, the epitome of Catholic liturgical music, and ends with the cadence figure known as the 'Dresden Amen', familiar from Wagner's later use of it as the 'Grail' motif in *Parsifal*. The solemnity of this introduction is further emphasized by the use of trombones, which are then kept in reserve until the symphony's finale.

The *Allegro con fuoco* is clearly meant to represent struggle, and has a rougher sound than we normally associate with Mendelssohn.

---

[1] Ludwig Rellstab: *Iris im Gebiete der Tonkunst*, 3/47 (23 November 1832), 187–8, quoted from: Ralph Larry Todd, *Mendelssohn Studies* (Cambridge, 1992), 160

[2] ibid.

In one account it is claimed that he orchestrated this movement in a curious and experimental way: vertically, rather than horizontally. That is, he wrote out each bar of the score from top to bottom, one bar per instrument, rather than by melodic line or by groups of instruments.

The central movements are not directly connected with the symphony's narrative idea, although the shadow of the 'Dresden Amen' can be traced in some of the melodic ideas. The second, despite its quick tempo marking, is not a real scherzo, but the sort of movement that Brahms might have called an intermezzo. In the third movement the first violins predominate with a melody that at times becomes the sort of instrumental recitative that strains towards vocal expression. Near the end there is a brief reminiscence of the first movement then, without a pause, a solo flute launches the finale with the first line of 'Ein' feste Burg ist unser Gott' (A mighty fortress is our God), the famous chorale with both words and music by Martin Luther. The flute is joined by other wind instruments in rich counterpoint, and the tempo quickens to an *Allegro maestoso* with strenuous fugal writing and a second subject that sounds very like a victory march. The symphony culminates with the apotheosis of 'Ein' feste Burg', a sound as thoroughly Protestant as any German Lutheran could wish for.

Andrew Huth

VORWORT

Zum ersten Mal erwähnt Mendelssohn die Sinfonie Nr. 5 in einem Brief, den er seiner Familie im September 1829 aus Wales schickte als sich sein siebenmonatiger Aufenthalt in Großbritannien, der ihn zu der Ouvertüre *Die Hebriden* und zur *Schottischen* Sinfonie inspiriert hatte, dem Ende näherte. Er beabsichtigte, etwas für die 300-Jahr-Feier des Augsburger Bekenntnisses zu komponieren, einem Schlüsselerlebnis der protestantischen Reformation: Am 25. Juni 1530 wurden dem katholischen Kaiser Karl V. 28 Artikel vorgelegt, die die Grundlage des lutherischen Glaubens herausstellten.

Einen konkreten Auftrag für eine Sinfonie gab es jedoch nicht und Mendelssohns jüdische Abstammung würde sich vielleicht nachteilig für ihn ausgewirkt haben, wenn eine musikalische Würdigung tatsächlich stattgefunden hätte. Obwohl er jedenfalls nach Berlin zurückkehrte und die Sinfonie mit gewohnter Schnelligkeit und Begeisterung im Mai 1830 beendete, begab sich fast unverzüglich auf eine lange Reise durch den Süden Deutschlands, durch Italien und Frankreich. Eine Aufführung unter der Leitung François-Antoine Habenecks zu Beginn des Jahres 1832 war geplant, doch die französischen Musiker verweigerten zum Ärger Mendelssohns die Mitwirkung, da ihnen das Werk zu reich an kontrapunktischen Elementen war und die Klänge zu wenig ihrem Geschmack entsprachen. Dies war auch im Wesentlichen die Reaktion des Berliner Dichters und Kritikers Ludwig Rellstab, nachdem Mendelssohn die Uraufführung am 15. November 1832 geleitet hatte. Rellstab war beeindruckt, aber räumte auch ein:

Lieber wäre es uns freilich, wenn der Componist nicht so viel auf colossale, als auf schöne Grundzüge hielte, wenn er nicht so überreich instrumentirte und endlich mehr den melodischen als den harmonischen, kühn combinirten Schönheiten das Übergewicht verstattete. Auch zeigt er uns selten einen heitern Himmel; fast immer stürmt oder gewittert es.[1]

In der seltsamen Art, in der sich Komponisten manchmal gegen ihre Werke wenden, unternahm Mendelssohn keine weiteren Bemühungen die Sinfonie anzupreisen oder zu veröffentlichen. Seine Haltung mag weniger in den musikalischen Qualitäten des Werks begründet sein als vielmehr in seiner strengen Auffassung darüber, was eine Sinfonie sein oder nicht sein sollte. Ein Hinweis findet sich in einer weiteren Bemerkung Rellstabs: „Es kann niemals die Aufgabe der Musik seyn, eine Begebenheit, die der reinen Welt des Gedankens fast allein angehört, auf sinnliche Weise darzustellen."[2] Der Sinfonie liegt ein eindeutig programmatisches, ja sogar erzählerisches Konzept zu Grunde, da es den Triumph des „aufgeklärten" Protestantismus über den „finsteren" Katholizismus repräsentiert. Was auch immer Mendelssohns religiöse Standpunkte waren – und wir wissen, dass er in dieser Hinsicht sehr liberal und tolerant war – seine musikalischen Vorstellungen sahen eine scharfe Trennung zwischen „illustrativer" und „purer" Musik vor und er dürfte sich wohl bewusst geworden sein, dass was einer Ouvertüre oder einem Werk mit einem Text in der Art eines Oratoriums angemessen ist, in einer Sinfonie, die sich nur mit abstrakten musikalischen Prozessen befassen sollte, fehl am Platz ist. Was auch immer hinter seinem Unbehagen steckte, es rechtfertigt wohl kaum seine überlieferte Bezeichnung des ersten Satzes als „ein dickes Tier mit Borsten" oder seinen angeblichen Wunsch, das ganze Stück zu verbrennen. Erst nach seinem Tod wurde die Sinfonie als Nummer fünf veröffentlicht, obwohl es genau genommen, nach der Reihenfolge der Komposition, die zweite Sinfonie ist.

[1] Ludwig Rellstab: *Iris im Gebiete der Tonkunst*, 3/47, 23. November 1832, S. 187f, zitiert nach Ralph Larry Todd: *Mendelssohn Studies*, Cambridge 1992, S. 160.
[2] Ebd.

Die Introduktion der Sinfonie wird in einer feierlichen Stimmung eröffnet, mit der Art Kontrapunkt, die zu Mendelssohns Zeit mit dem Stil Palestrinas, dem Inbegriff der katholischen liturgischen Musik, in Verbindung gebracht wurde; sie schließt mit einer kadenziellen Figur, die als das „Dresdner Amen" bekannt ist, welche wiederum durch Wagners späteren Gebrauch als „Grals"-Motiv in *Parsifal* geläufig werden sollte. Die Feierlichkeit dieser Introduktion wird darüber hinaus durch den Einsatz von Posaunen betont, die dann erst wieder im Finale der Sinfonie erklingen.

Das *Allegro con fuoco* soll einen Kampf darstellen und erscheint in einem stürmischeren Ton als wir normalerweise von Mendelssohn erwarten würden. In einer Darstellung wird behauptet, dass er diesen Satz auf eine seltsame und experimentelle Art instrumentiert hat: eher vertikal als horizontal. Das heißt, anstelle von Melodielinien oder Instrumentengruppen notierte er jeden Takt der Partitur von oben nach unten aus, jeweils einen Takt pro Instrument.

Die zentralen Sätze sind nicht unmittelbar mit dem erzählerischen Konzept der Sinfonie verbunden, obwohl der Schatten des „Dresdner Amen" in einigen melodischen Einfällen ausfindig gemacht werden kann. Der zweite Satz ist, trotz seiner schnellen Tempobezeichnung, kein wirkliches Scherzo, sondern die Art von Satz, die Brahms wohl als Intermezzo bezeichnet hätte. Im dritten Satz herrschen die ersten Violinen vor mit einer Melodie, die sich zeitweise zu einer Art Instrumentalrezitativ entwickelt, das in Richtung vokaler Ausdrucksweise drängt. Kurz vor dem Ende findet sich eine knappe Reminiszenz an den ersten Satz; ohne Pause führt die Soloflöte mit der ersten Zeile von „Ein' feste Burg ist unser Gott", dem berühmten Choral mit Text und Musik von Martin Luther, in das Finale ein. Weitere Blasinstrumente stimmen mit reichlich Kontrapunkt ein, und das Tempo beschleunigt sich zu einem *Allegro maestoso* mit energisch fugaler Setzweise und einem zweiten Thema, das sehr nach einem Siegesmarsch klingt. Die Sinfonie gipfelt in einer Apotheose von „Ein' feste Burg", einem Klang, so uneingeschränkt protestantisch wie es sich jeder deutsche Lutheraner nur wünschen konnte.

Andrew Huth
Übersetzung: Sandra Borzikowski

SYMPHONY No. 5
'Reformation'

Felix Mendelssohn Bartholdy
(1809–1847)
Op. 107

I. Andante

© 2015 Ernst Eulenburg Ltd, London
and Ernst Eulenburg & Co GmbH, Mainz

4

Allegro con fuoco.

6

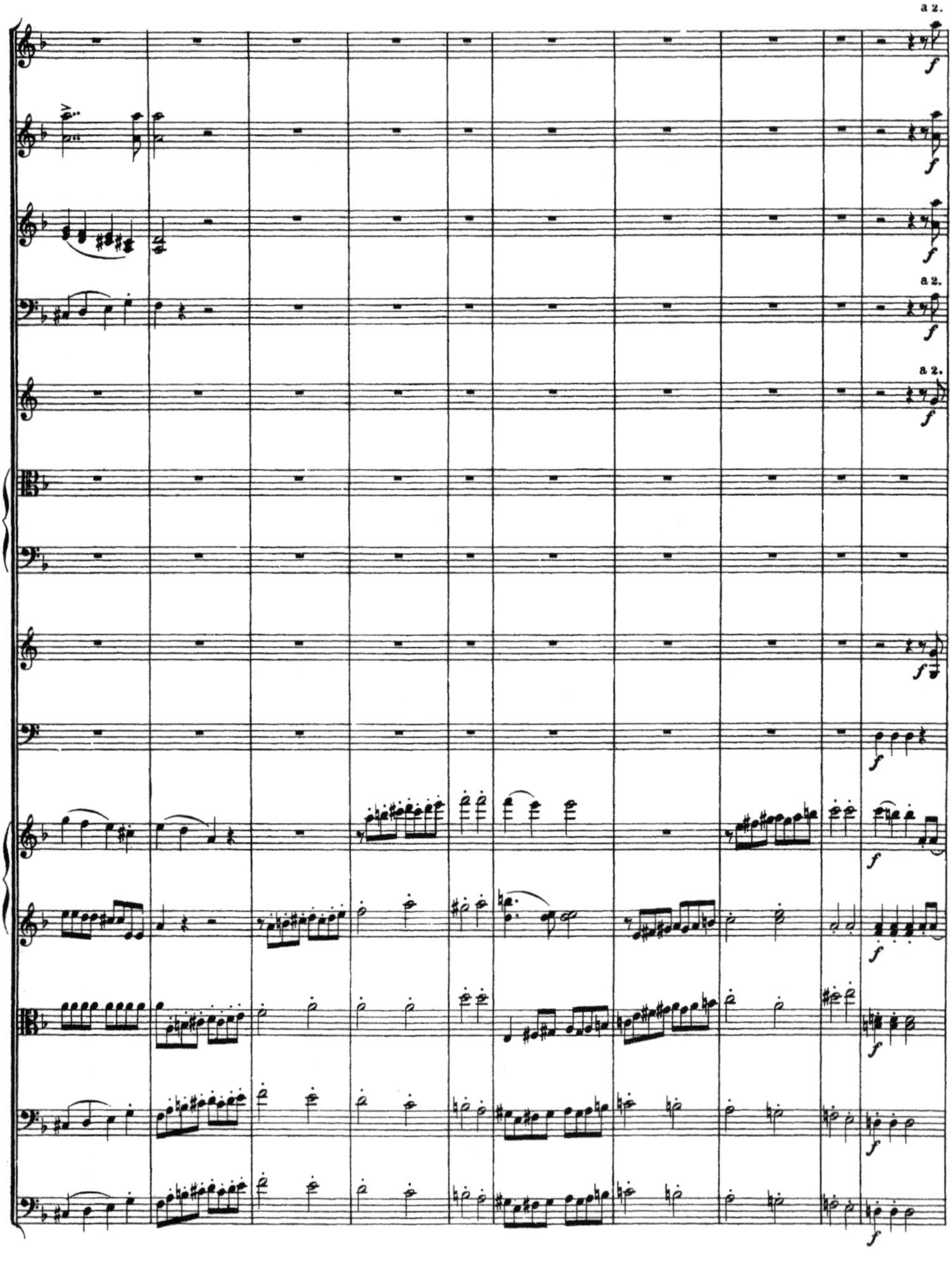
a 2.
f
f
f
a 2.
f
a 2.
f
f
f
f
f
f
f
f

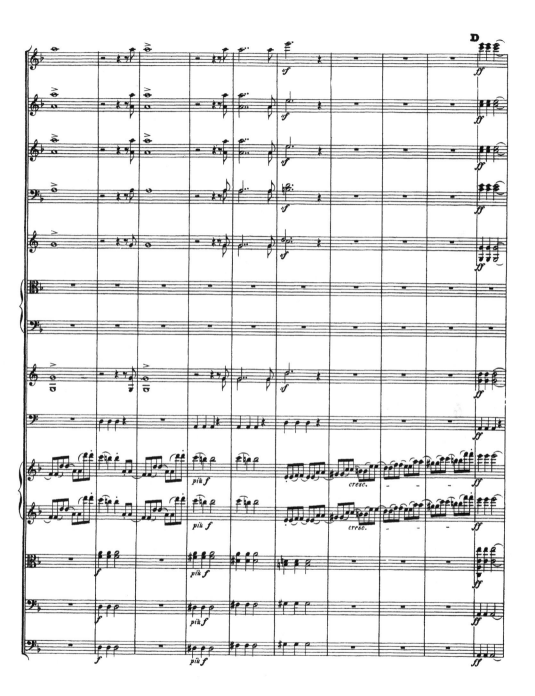

32

Andante come I.　　meno Allegro come I.

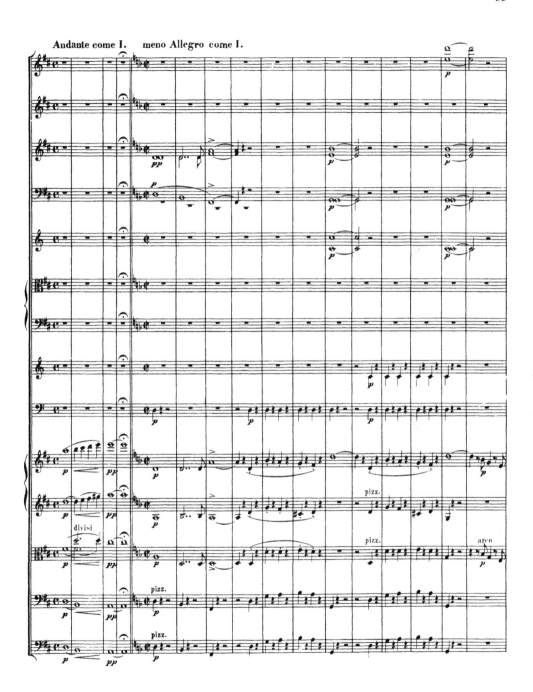

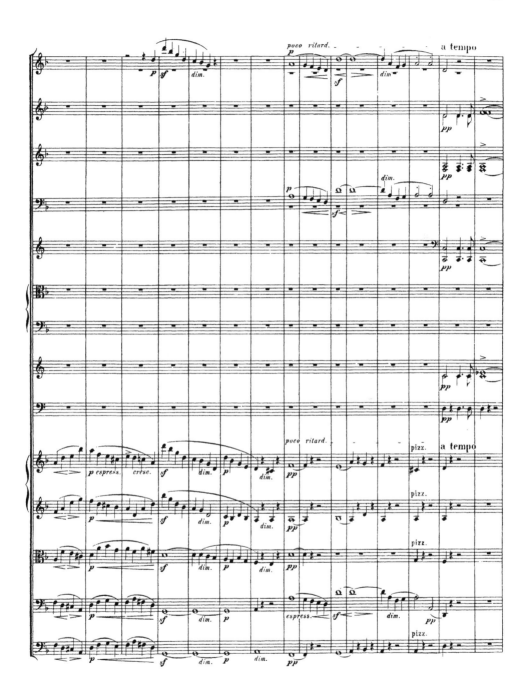

II. Allegro vivace

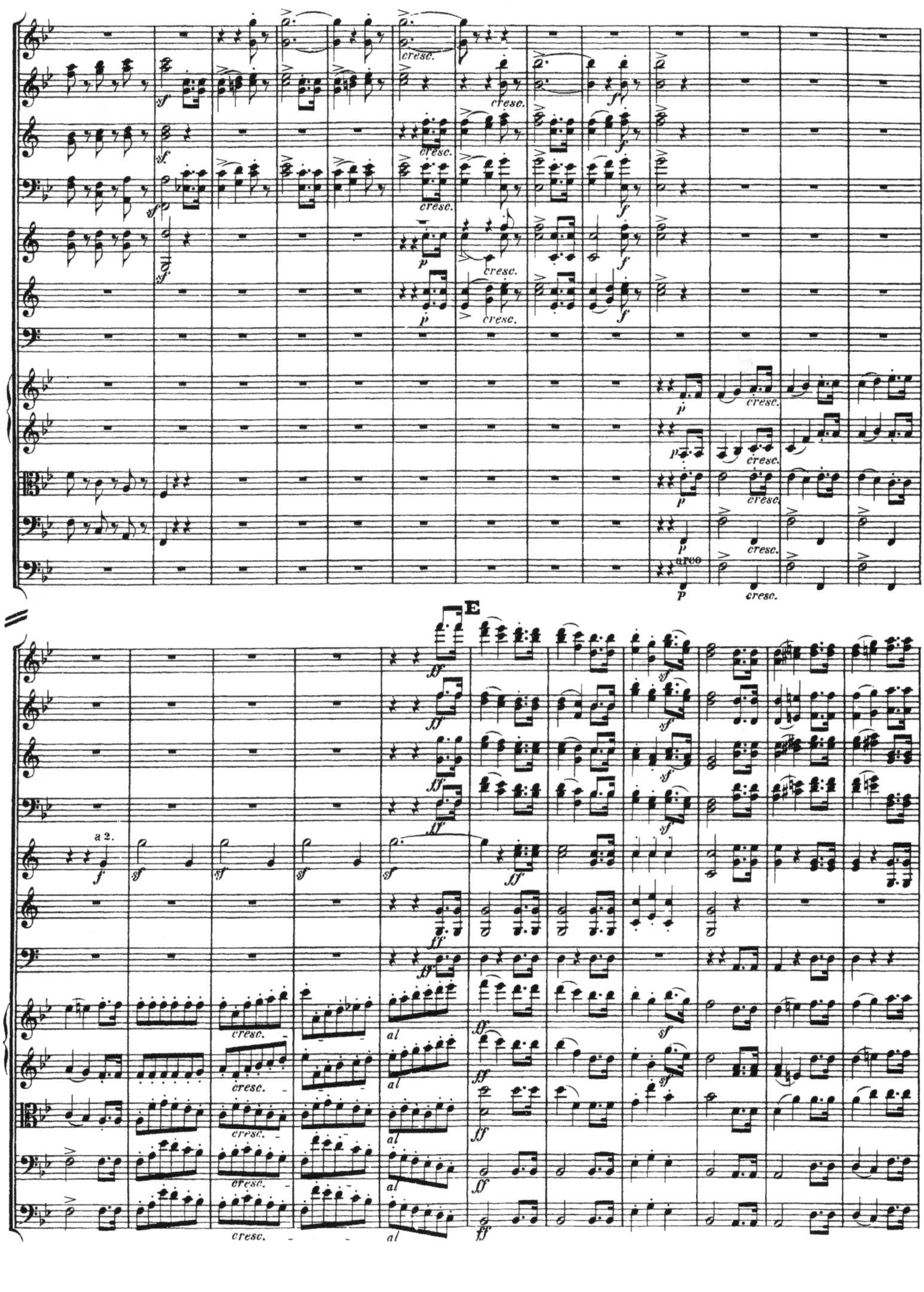
cresc.
sf
p
f
arco
E
a 2.
ff
al

F

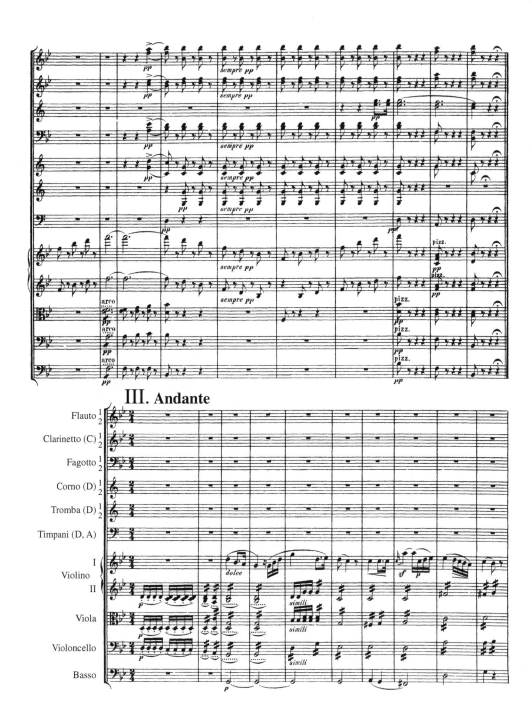

III. Andante

Flauto 1/2

Clarinetto (C) 1/2

Fagotto 1/2

Corno (D) 1/2

Tromba (D) 1/2

Timpani (D, A)

Violino I

Violino II

Viola

Violoncello

Basso

IV. Chorale: Ein' feste Burg ist unser Gott
Andante con moto

Allegro vivace.

Allegro maestoso.

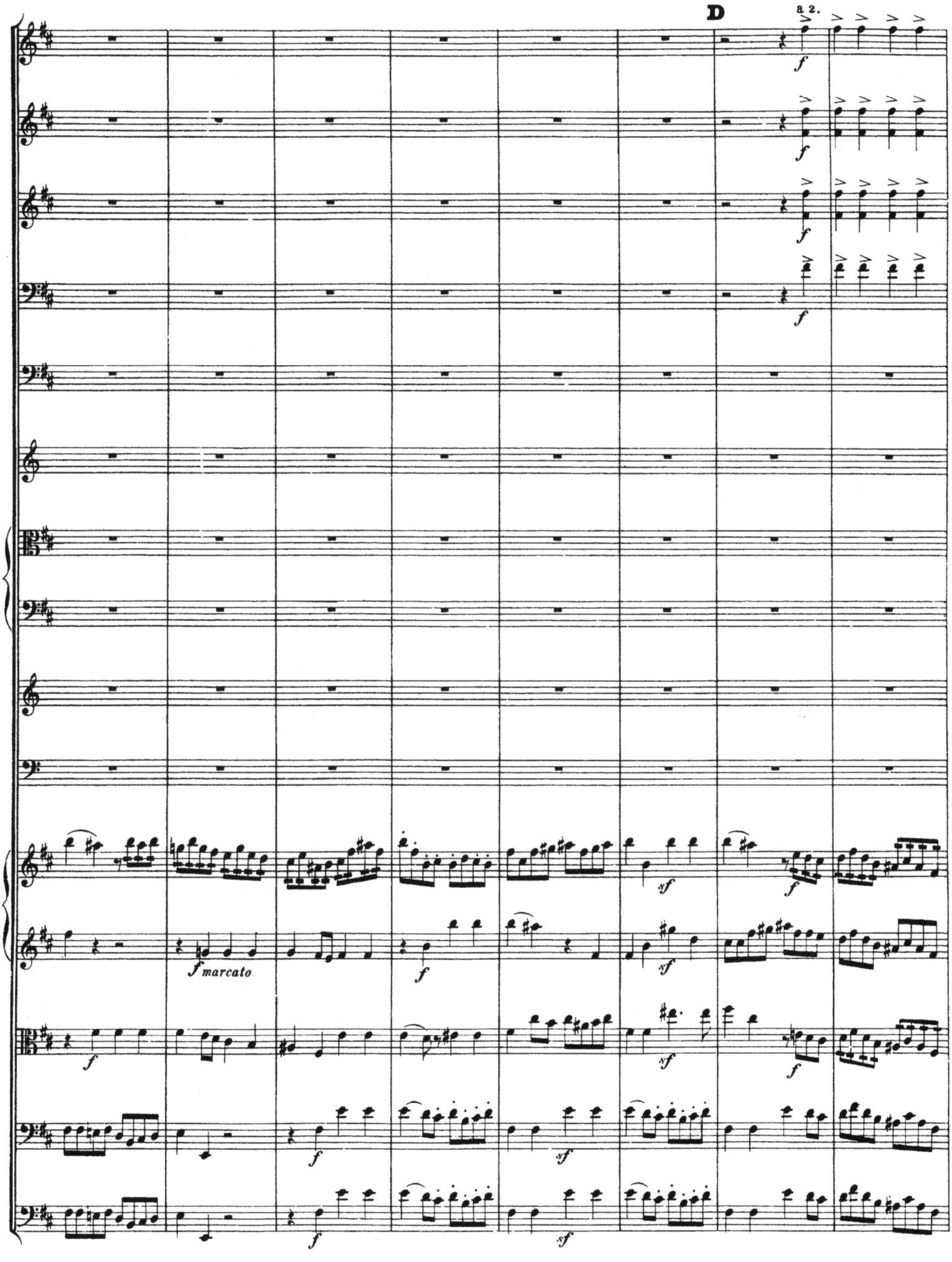
D
a 2.
f marcato
sf

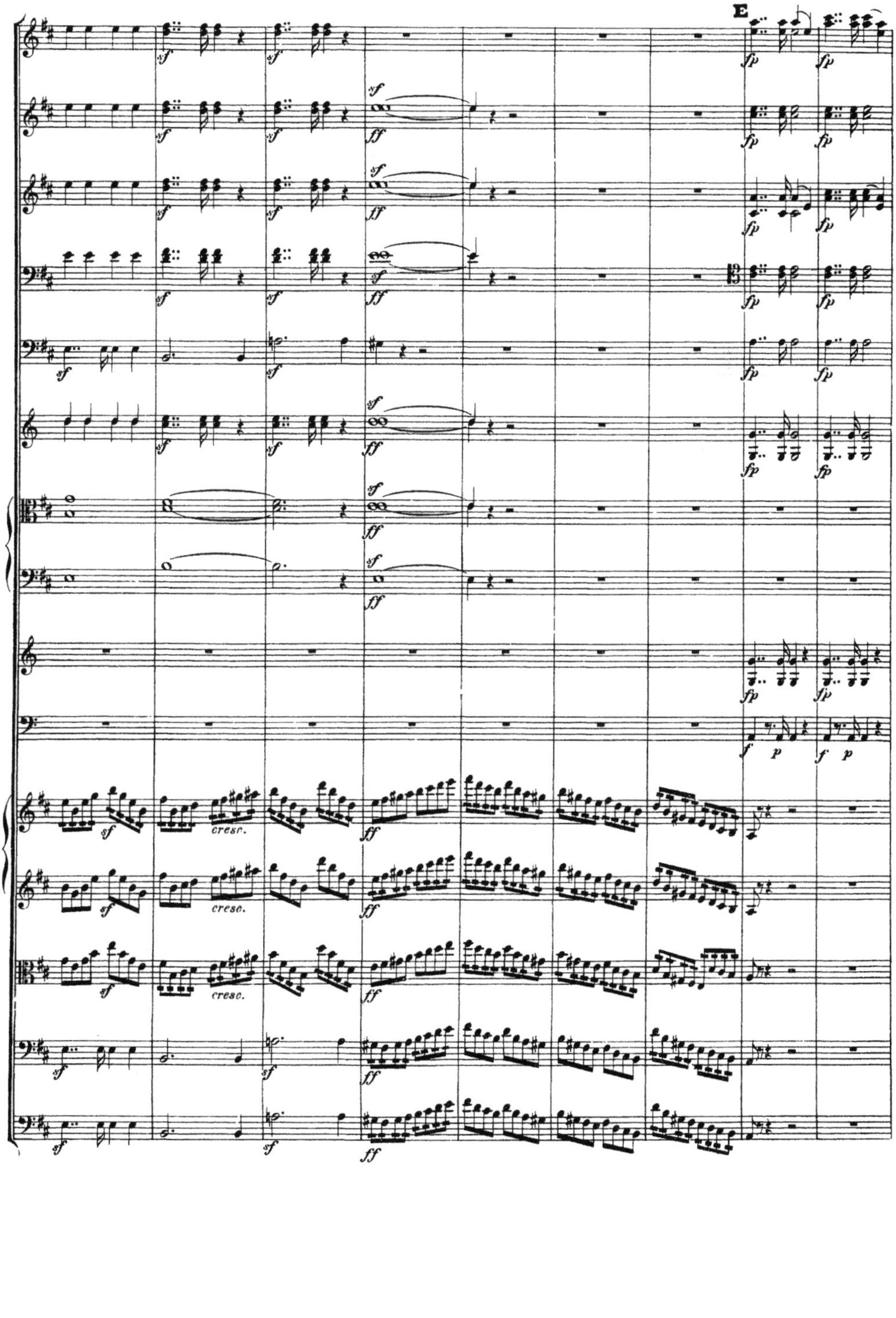
E
sf
ff
fp
f
p
cresc.

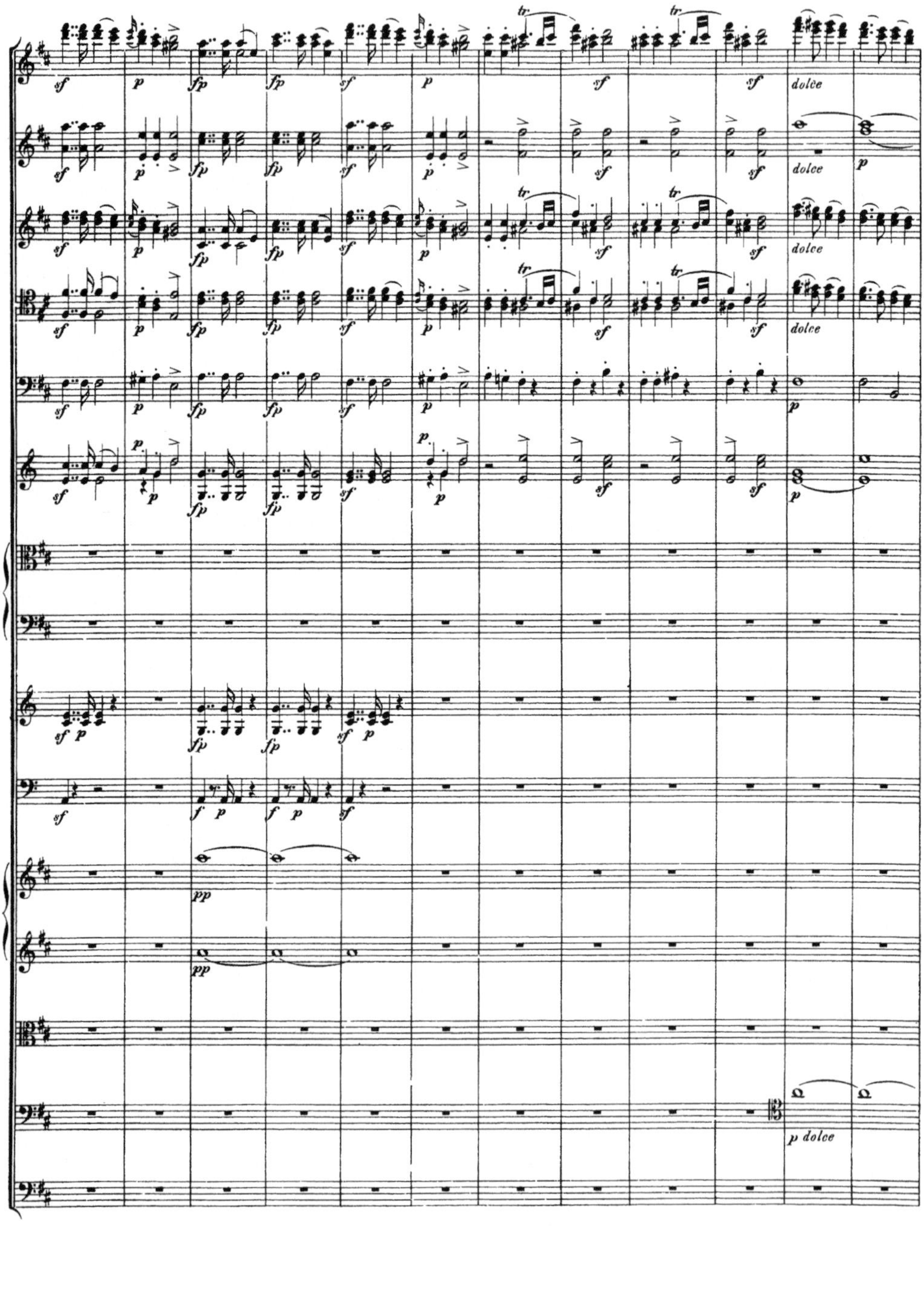

sf
p
fp
tr
dolce
pp
f
p dolce

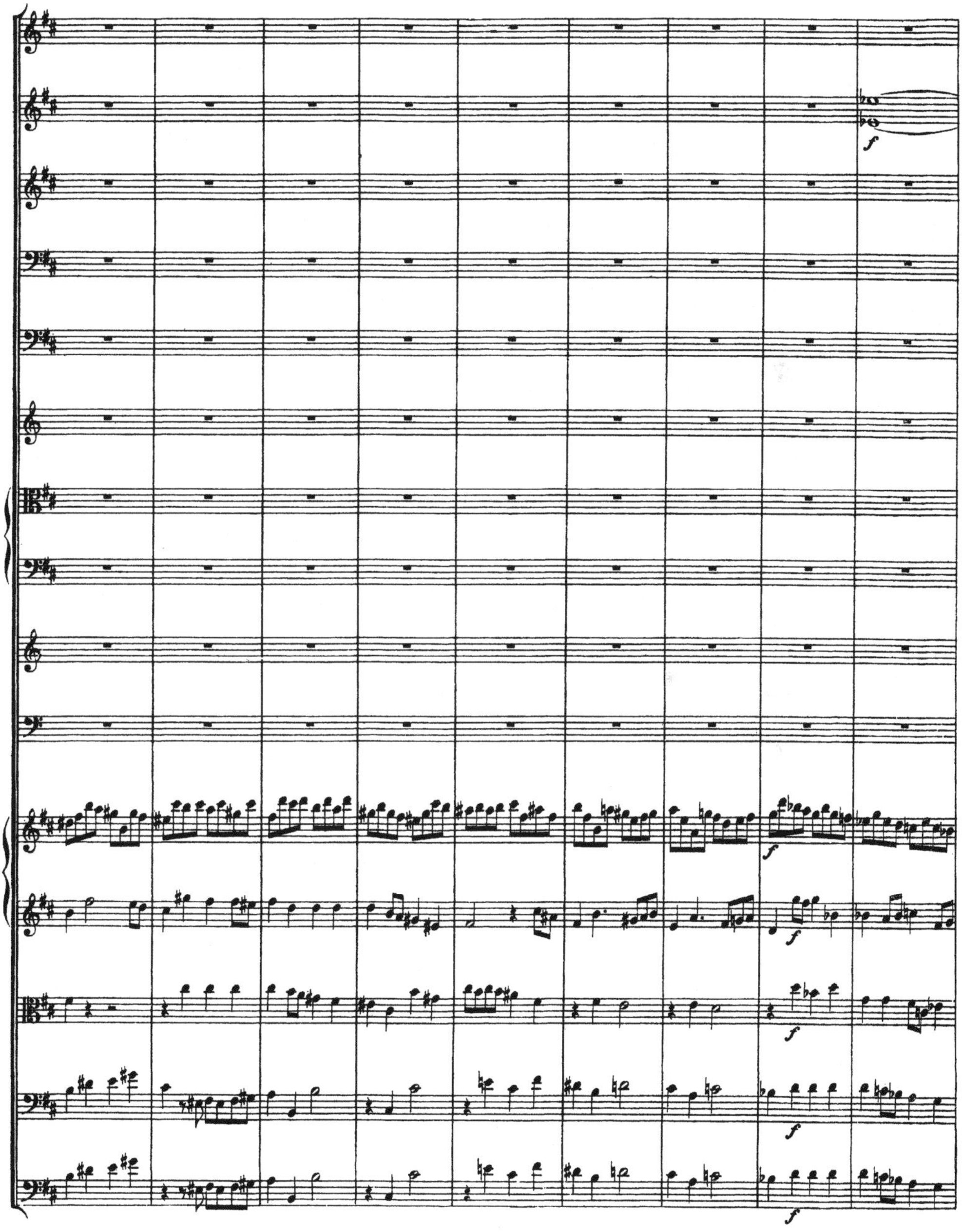
f

M
Più animato poco a poco.

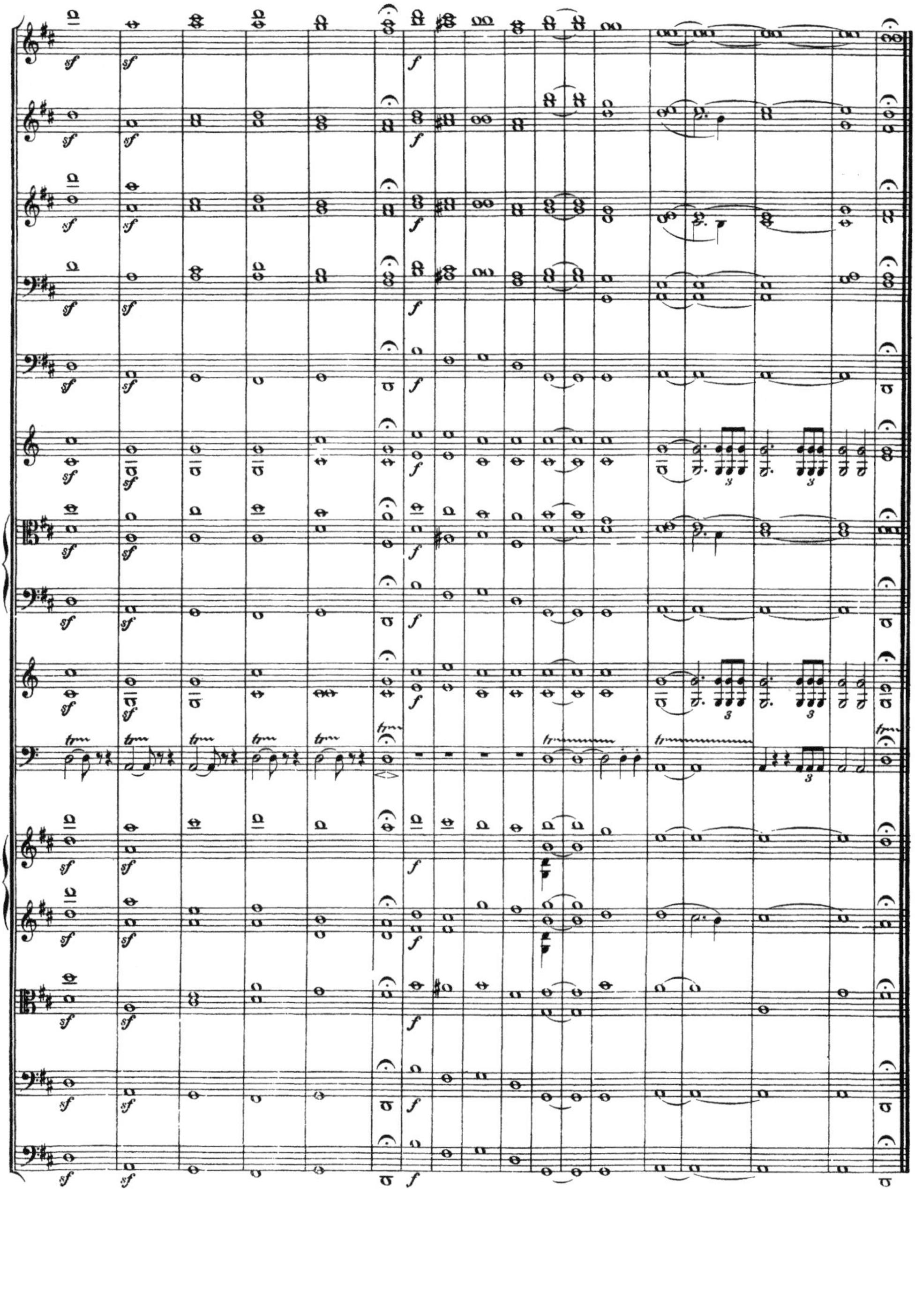
sf
f
tr